Livin' ina Aucklan'

CENTRAL

Passing Young's Lane

As the early morning train pulls out
Of Newmarket Station it dives down towards Auckland

Towards another working day: The bells ring
And the warning lights flash at Young's Lane

I look indifferently out the window
Expecting to see nothing other than dark-grey skies

To my right a shaft of golden light
Transforms the otherwise sullen landscape

Beyond the marshes and swamps of Orakei
Straight down the Gulf I see Waiheke

Where you two moved to the other day
Waiheke is the place where the light is strongest

Suddenly the train lurches to the left
We enter the Parnell Tunnel plunged into darkness

30 cent inner-city fare

Hop on the big yellow
        banana bus
and go from station to stop to stop
initial surge of power throws you –
back, back as banana on wheels
pushes forward past phoenix palms
and then flows around what was
once a beach – now a road
into, but past also anzac beach head
then, the battle been fought, into the mainstream
maelstrom to follow local custom
left, through the turquoise northern shadow – great!
the pacific (south) lost now in large seas
and the queen lies spread-eagled and eager
to engulf all-comers . . .
up you go and she is before you and following
as you move in fits and starts
– a sexual epileptic
fish tank vision of the people
and the crane-like cranes hanging their long
necks over building tops to check your progress
as you check their progress at a red light

a swarm of people descends and then moves
– as you move . . .
bathed in a golden glow the hint of the wide
open country-side
the banana moves up and up but never away
now the fantasy movie is all but finished
but the real illusion continues
– they are building more of them and more of them
and just when you think you might get lost
forever in the orgasmic firmament
     going up further and faster
     than you can ever remember
the banana bends to the right, missing the sky
          by inches

and slows
     slows to reveal human faces
laughing and sad, moving and still in K-Rd
time to hop off the big yellow
        banana bus!

The Craic, the Kai, and the Whiskey
(71st memorial of the Easter Uprising) for Karen Urale

What's happening and where!
It's the place and it's the drinking
Went to the Eden Terrace factory
Kissed my love by the wall, but it's only a song
        and then (will we go ta midnight mass or no?)
In the pub talkin' and drinkin'
Drivin' through the night
- the moon rises, clouds are drifting
And everywhere the city grows and moves
(Thinkin' about the girl I just met)
So it's off with the top of the Tullamore Dew
And down it goes
Firing up the organs like a mainline steam engine
Is it yourself? Who knows -
As all the constraints of reason
And morality get lost in
The craic, the kai, and the whiskey
It's a wild unremembered drive
Through the Balmoral night
- I awake in the morning
To a vision of O'Donnell driving
Straight towards a Concrete Wall

Thursday Night at the Naval and Family

Listening, looking, thinking and remembering

First, listening to the island band
        same old songs week after week
        the rhythm moves my feet
        and the drink and smiles
        make me feel like I'm sort of at home
        the voices and the words
        foreign and familiar

Looking out the window at O'Malley's Corner
        and following with my eyes
        past other Karangahape Road neons
        up to the lines of old Auckland roof-tops and sunset sky
        then inside seeing
        all the pretty girls dancing
        talking and singing and smoking cigarettes

Thinking why am I here and
        why do I keep coming to this place
        where some nights I'm the only local
        although I can't see that
        and no-one else seems to notice
        and the foreigner I've been all my life
        doesn't exist here

And remembering the Pacific Island music
        my mother used to play on the gramophone
        and the Pacific Island woman
        who shared my life
        and dreams for a short while
        - as the music wafts over me like waves
        I stare into my glass with anger at separation

Way to Work, Way to Go!

The whoosh of smoke
From the car in front's exhaust
Covers our windscreen and
We drive blindly past Penrose Railway Station

Seems funny to pick up and
Pay money for sand in bags
From a Mount Wellington factory floor
With the smell of a fresh Westfield kill filling the morning air

We hit the motorway northward
Towards the city – across
The Newmarket Viaduct with
Eurythmic music going as loud as we are fast – crazy!

The drive of the dead –
Through Grafton Graveyard
Traffic to the right, to the left
It's underneath you, and it's over the top!

Then down to the oil installations
The noise and smell, the sea and sky
And the sand we bought
Now blasting through a nozzle
Knocking off last generation's paint
Off petrol pipelines as the sun beats down hard

WEST

Rock and Cave

at Whatipu

the caves are hollow

and hidden

no light or

life can be seen in

these solitary places

and then

the heads of the Western

Manukau jut out

Buffeted, undermined

by winds and

by rain and salt water

if you

stand on the beach

feeling the force of the elements

and look

up to the safety and

darkness of the caves

then decide

on te wahi moemoeä, shadows

and the half-life

or stand strong, Kia Kaha,

and be shaped and eroded

down to the last pebble of existence

Livin' ina Aucklan'

all too soon it is over
stepping down on to the platform
(an almost perfect concrete curve of old-world technology)
and watching the train move away towards the west
like a memory of love

a railway is the most melancholy of transport modes
and when you are aboard
the motion is one of subtle love-making
– as the train pulls out
from the station you stepped down at . . .

it is your lover leaving, rolling down the track

all this on a two minute trip to Avondale
but I defend the suburban services
saying romance is not confined to the Orient Express
and Mount Albert is as important as Montmartre
if you live there

once new and unknown
love is like a railway ticket held in my hand
but it has been clipped
as I stand alone on wind-swept Avondale platform
                    watching the train pull out of the station, I . . .

Morningside Station

bright blue sky in
            mid-winter warmth

sun beats down and
            heats the station seat

I sit looking at a red
            light in the distance

waiting for it to turn green
            the train ain't far away

its whistle blowing down
            the line as it approaches

the just out of sight bridge
            over New North Road

gum trees glisten among
        single-storey factories

their blue shimmer heightens
        the fine-edged colours

graffiti gangs battle on walls
        with slogans that defy each other

the power of television images
        proven by these

New York subway copy-cats
        and I mean cats

NORTH

Torbay! Torbay! Torbay!

It's around and around goes the bus
Out of sight of the sea
This suburb seems to go on and on
As we walk together to my sister's house
Along a white concrete path

The white child of my sister
Looks at the dark woman I am with
As though she is a creature
From another island or time –
Afterwards she tells me what I know

So near to the sea, the sound
Is almost there, like inside a shell
And over the bridge inside a bus
We return to the city together
Carelessly we go to dinner or a movie

Next time I go to Torbay I am alone
The same bus, same streets
Same suburban sounds, near the sea
I am in another island or time
And I am alone, like the sound inside a shell

Takapuna: buy the sea
(America's Cup review, 1986 – 87)

The whole country
Acted like the 'Olde Mug' –
The peasants again duped
By the glittering gold phrases
Of the middle-class gentry

Television pirates:
Protectors of the public mind
And pilferers of the public purse
Nightly filled our hedonistic heads
With age-old delusions

"Both yachts will be
looking for real estate –
but the leader's got the edge".
And it was the same on land
As in the inane commentary box

If you told someone
You owned an underwater acre
Off the coast of Whangaparoa or
Takapuna, or Milford, you would have
Made a million for you overnight

But now in the cold grey dawn
Of falling shares and broken illusions
We look and see El Dorado and the Golden Calf
Are just another brick shit-house, and
The America's Cup is back where it belongs

Torbay Revisited

went   this
time in a car
        white car

into the
monochrome suburb
        white suburb

inside the
kids watched TV
        white television

and when
number two child
        white-haired

looked up
and saw
my black
hair and
black beard
he was
afraid and
went crying
to mummy
- like
he'd never
seen anything
dark in
his life
before . . .

SOUTH

Untitled

looking from the train window
towards Mangere Bridge
between a redundant Southdown
                freezing works
and long ago re-aligned Otahuhu Station

                                    at sundown

see the beauty of the natural cliffs

                                    of the harbour heads

reflected in the stillness
of the Manukau Harbour
as shades of purple
enhance the land and water
the train pulls southward out of Westfield

A Penrose Pineapple
(for David Eggleton)

industrial grey
backgrounds this
red-blue bordered
painting as though
some punk Gaugin
gotta hold of
the notion that
the Pacific Ocean
needed some
sorta expression
for its time and place
industrio-tropical
and a real
Penrose high is
resultant, subject to
flecked fruit
red – yellow – green
zig-zag jagged
edges behind which
lies Christmas Island
Happy New Year
on Mururoa
and the pineapple
is number one fruit
on the menu at
Atomic Café, Tokyo
branch-line to
Onehunga via Te Papapa

bullet train, bomb train
no time (fragmented)
like the present
shunted reality
nuclear free, unclear future
"Bravo! Bravo!" its
the U.S. Marshall Islands
playing in the Pacific basin
and the Penrose pineapple
says enjoy your
full half-life

Otara – have a Banana

coming back from the Papatoetoe pub
towards Otara in a Japanese car made for two
I am lolling like a sea-lion in the back

the little car turns the corner too quickly and as
I put my hand out instinctively to stop the roll, it moves into outer-space as the
window shatters on the road

laughing from shock as we cross the motorway overbridge
I see the clouds and sky more clearly with no window
and the fresh breeze quickens my slight hysteria

we pull into the large asphalt covered carpark
which on weekends transforms into a busy market place
but now is only populated by tin ghosts on wheels

leaving my friends I head towards the town-centre
where people shop and smile and talk, listen to music
and the aiitu of you is around every corner

sitting in a cafe I order coffee and a roll
in a gravel-syrup voice, thinking Tom Waits for no-one
as another mother joins the endless Post Office queue

Russian Roulette

'привет tovarisch'
'Hello comrade,' I reply
as she greets me off the train at Ellerslie station
It is not the stiff, formal handshake
but rather the playful shake of her head
that I notice . . .

sending her hair running after the wind
as we walk together
from the platform
                    towards our usual meeting place

I order two cups of black, strong coffee -
We sit silent for a short time
Then, leaning forward, she asks softly
'The tapes. Have you got the tapes, Comrade?'
'As always,' I reply
'хороший' she seems relieved
as I hand her a small package
                    wrapped like a lover's gift

We talk quietly with easy familiarity
until her eye catches the clock
and she rises and there is tension in the air
                    as there is each week when we part

'The factory, I'm late for the factory!'
she cries ...
we gather our things and walk fast around
around and around the circular walk-way
which leads from the road to the rail overbridge
the motorway sounds drown our goodbyes

'Mission completed' I think to myself
- as I board the train I glimpse her
standing on the foot bridge waving and calling out . . .

прощание, I've just fired
another shot -
          your turn comrade'

EAST

Remuera Dreamtime
(for Maria)

Its walking down the road
Where the hedges and the fences
Loom tall, the trees are tall
Beautiful and stilted

The light is the evening
Colours in the unmoving silence
It's the dream and it's the time
Of day and of life

Mercedes and copulating dogs
Are the only people on the street
It doesn't go near them
Because they get angry

And then at night the
Sharp sound of husband
And wife fighting, baying
Like dingoes in the dark

It rained in the morning
And the bus could be heard
Moving and shifting further down
Somebody's disturbed the Rainbow Serpent . . .

from its sleep in the deep waterhole

Pakuranga Lemonade
(Winter 1986)

put two lemons in a paper bag
add some brown sugar to taste and then ...
fill the bag up with water
quickly, before the bag gets soggy, lie it on the ground
and stamp on it as hard as possible with one foot,
this recipe is guaranteed to give you at least one wet leg
and is quite undrinkable
a tree which loved lemons gave it to me
lemons had been the fruit
now this tree had been sacrificed
so that people could have a swimming pool
thick lumps of heavy, dead clay
had clogged its roots and killed its will
death came gradually –

the Polynesian labourer was the only one to see it
because people of Pakuranga had walked by him
as though he was a dead tree in their suburb
and in their white fright they saw him
as a leafless, ugly vision of wild threat
but he looked at the lemon tree and its outstretched branches
and saw that his brown skin matched the brown bark
so that as he lifted shovel load after shovel load
his dreams were of coconut trees and bright flowers
and catching fish in the sea of his island home of light
and colourful birds,
meanwhile, the other people
kept an eye on the progress of the hole in the ground

Okahu Bay

Dark night, wind off the harbour
Once you approach the sand
The pohutukawa trees surround you
The moon, cut in half and half-hidden by clouds
Provides the only natural light
Each wave that laps at your feet
Has reached you from eternity
The darkness of self - of unremembered soul
The night within embraces my vision
The sadness of each memory
Is like each wave of water
Together they make a flood of tears
Which drown the cries of the heart
This evening you were the moon to me
The only pure light in a life of shadows
Like the moon you too hid behind a veil
Showing light enough for life, but not for love
After a time we left for Okahu Bay
Broke through the line of pohutukawa
I let you walk ahead so you would not see me
Kneel, then kiss the ground,
The ground of my childhood, the ground of my life

Okahu
(as translated by Jean Wikiriwhi)

Kua pouri, ka pupuhi te hau
Mai i te moana,
Hurihuri nga pohutukawa,
Te Marama hangere, kua ahua ngaro i te kapua
Ko tenei anake te maramatanga,
Ke ata papakihia mai e nga ngaru a wae
Ka te pouri au, kua wareware te ngakau,
Ko te po kei te awhi i taku kitenga,
Te aroha ki tena ki tena,
Pera ki ia ngaru o te wai,
Hui katoa, ka heke te manawa,
I tenei ahiahi ko koe
Te marama ki ahau
Ko kou te maramatanga, i tenei ao pouri,
Pera i te marama kahuna kou i
Ko te maramatanga hei oranga, kaore mo te aroha
A, ka wehe mai i Okahu
Ka mahue nga pohutukawa,
Ko koe i mua, kia kore koe e kite i ahau
Ka tuturi, ka kihi i te one,
Ko te one o taku tamarikitanga,
          to one o taku oranga ...

6.15 Waiheke Ferry to Auckland, Wednesday 20 July, 1983

The line of the low hill undulates
As I keep my head still
And let the boat do all the . . .
                   movement

Darkness shrouds my journey but
There is light
In the sky the stars and the moon shine like pearls
Waves break along the bow
White foam almost frozen by the cold
I am in tune with the natural melancholy
I move like an iceberg from shore to shore

For me this is the end of journey and beginning
Dressed in black, I resign
For years I have traveled in pursuit
You made sure I was always one step behind
Covered your trail whenever I got close

From the safety and calm of the bay
The ferry now sails into open waters

Rangitoto reminds me of you
Looks the same from any angle
Except close-up
But the sky is not on fire tonight
And, if I am alight it is with the fire of ice

Two lovers come on deck
They feel the chill in the night air
When they turn and see me, dark and still
Perhaps they feel another chill . . .
                        they leave for the cabin
This evening takes on a rare quality
This boat could be anywhere
                        if it weren't so cold
We might be travelling from
                        one Greek Isle to another
And I might be anyone
                        instead of thinking of you
I could be in the warm arms of a lover . . .
But I wouldn't have it any other way
Austerity has a beauty all its own

I try to imagine from which position
North Head was named
Why not South Head etc
You are fading from me
I am being engulfed by the lights
                        and distractions of the city
I try to think of why I love you
But things are moving too fast
                        the boat is making up lost time
                        the boat is making up lost time
With Auckland upon us people emerge from inside
I find I am talking to someone
                        he has been chopping trees at his section

My friend who waits for me on the wharf
Greets me with a jovial "Hello sailor!"
Immediately I get ashore we go to a pub
Where I down a double whiskey to break the ice

Auckland Revisited

i

Britomart, steel and glass
Huge flow of water above
Nestled in the ceiling
And a feeling that
       its not just me that has arrived
The city is also now focused
Large nikau palms
Offer internal calm
I feel like singing
       . . . a psalm
In this new transport cathedral

ii

Outside the station
The buses wait
The heavy stone of the once CPO
Now seems light
       almost ethereal
And across the way
The ferries bob and rhyme
To the Poet of the Harbour's time
Who dreams of Jeanie: Rising Sun
       . . . and shine
Or in lite-brown ale and air

iii

Travelling towards
The past of Ponsonby
No longer on a big, yellow, bendy
Banana, wending through
       the Queen's grand canyon
Spread-eagled, inviting all comers
But on a Link
Bus as it slinks
Like a silvery shadow
       . . . I think
Upon safe-sex allegations

K'Rd, looking at O'Malley's Corner
Listening to the talking bus
'Next Stop . . .' and thinking
About the time I'm remembering
      the Naval and Family
Which still looks beautiful, decrepit
And I'm remembering also
The song we sang, although
About another Samoan woman
      . . . we sang slow
In perfect harmony of reggae off-beat

Sitting in Old Ivan's café
Now new not-Ivan's
Everything is the same
But totally unrecognisable
      especially the food
And the wine. What! Wine! In Ivan's!!!
Oh, this could never be
Where's me old cup of tea?
And mince on toast
      . . . dear me
What happened to the Revolution?

Not far along the road
Where Herman painted other artists
And wrote 'In Praise of Koba'
In Margaret Street to be precise
      number eight
Once offered to me for two thousand dollars
Nowadays tarted-up, gentrified
Going along for the ride
The Bohemian new rich
      . . . now decide
Good art by its price tag

Past the old university goes
The silver-tongued linx
Where we used to sit in B28
Thinking about those B52s
        over Vietnam
Now they're over Afghanistan
Dropping their liberating load
On Mohamed, not Charlie
So it seems fairly
Apt that Khyber Pass
        . . . is clearly
The next stop after Symonds Street

Old Newmarket, where Sharpo
The silent voice of Marxism, meets
Bland footpath commercialism
Remembering waiting for Dado
        outside the pub
In back-streets of memory
My mind now wanders
And in those thoughts, wonders
How things might have been if . . .
        . . . ah! Life squanders
And I've got another train to catch

Casting a glance down-hill
Towards Young's Lane with its Bells
And Lights and the train's Hooter
Blasts as it backs along
        the embankment
Before heading westward
Stopping at the new Boston Road Station
Next to the prison, where, with some indignation
I recall visiting my father, who out of a certain
        . . . sense of desperation
Stole money. But the train moves on and away

X

Eden Terrace factories
Show their back view, like
They forget I used to work there
Making stove elements every day, plus
          two nights a week
And Saturday mornings over-time
Also four nights night-school
No wonder I'm such a fool
- the back of Kingsland shops
          . . . where every tool
Imaginable is employed by track-gang workers

xi

Double-tracking to the west
From Parimoana memories
Across the just out of sight
Bridge, Morningside where
          gum trees glisten
And graffiti gangs battle it out
And the poet's penis bursts
Through the roof, what's worse
Is this pain in here, too much of
          . . . nothing hurts
Says the New York Subway copy-cats

xii

Mount Albert to Avondale
Then we are heading down into real
Wild Westie country, where
A jokes a joke for all that
          then its no joke
But a cruel irony. One job I had was
Writing the history of the cemetery
Out here on the hill at Waikumete
Where my mother, father, and sister
          . . . lie under a tree
But none have stones to say which one

A forest of houses
Made by a forest of trees
Has sprung up between
Henderson and Ranui since
        my last visit
A miracle has occurred also
They have turned wine
Into art, which is fine
Although slightly run-down
        . . . Corban's estate in time
Has become Asid-Free and Art Gallery-fied

Quick turnaround at the bunker
Station of Waitakere
Then the train follows back
Whence it came
        the New North Road
Bridge is being doubled in reverse
And old Newmarket Station is worse
For wear and now un-used
        . . . its like some curse
Has descended, even at Remuera

But there are some compensations
Accompanying the new order
Greenlane is a station again
No longer just a coal pit
        as we head rail-south
Past the industrial Penrose pineapple
And long-redundant on-fire Southdown works
A no longer still-standing shell, the train jerks
To a halt, waiting for a cross-over shunt at Westfield
        . . . which lurks
Just beyond the Otahuhu works as the points change

xvi

Because this is an express
It is a clear run to Papakura
Through lazy Mangere afternoon
And Papatoetoe and Manurewa
        then another changeover back
And this time we take the points
At Westfield, into the Orakei Deviation
With a certain sense of elation
I am homeward bound, I wish I was
        . . . the source of creation
So as to recreate the past and its sorrows

xvii

A city of empty containers
Stacked several stories high
Has hidden
Nay, obliterated
        old Tamaki Station
Where my own life was prematurely
Almost ended, when I was a child
Running free and wild
I pulled ahead of my again pregnant mother
        . . . and fell onto the rails
As the guard gave the signal for the driver to go

xviii

Following the route where a cursed highway
Will no longer go
Through G.I., Meadowbank, and looking
Up, I see the haunts of Orakei
        of my boyhood
The horses still run
In paddocks by the old school
We travel the rail causeway, past Parnell Pool
And the bay of Judges, where
        . . . we kept cool
All day, all summer long

xix

Next day we are downtown
Upping the ante above the city
In the Sky Tower
Walking on glass and losing
       on the Black Jack
The view is almost as good
As being up Mount Eden
Or Mount Albert, when
I lived out west we would play
    . . . cricket there, then
Zoom around town, chauffeured in a Mercedes by Benito

xx

On the Devonport Ferry
The waves are choppy
As we watch Auckland
City recede into
      the distance
My sister picks us up as we get off the bus
At Takapuna. After dinner
She drives back through thinner
Evening traffic to Ponsonby
    . . . and the inner
City looks bright and rain washed

xxi

Leaving next day by car
Heading down the early night motorway
From Mangere Bridge where
We pick up a disputed art work
      south-east of Bombay
We get lost on dark, unknown roads
Trying to find Paddy of Patamahoe
In the back roads near Pukekohe
Criss-crossing the Glenbrook railway line
    . . . after we have a moe
We are early morning, southward bound towards Kapiti